Slimy

Written by Jo Windsor

Rigby

This slug has
a slimy skin.

slug

This snail has
a slimy skin.

snail

This worm has
a slimy skin.

worm

This fish has
a slimy skin.

fish

This frog has
a slimy skin.

frog

This frog has
a slimy skin, too.

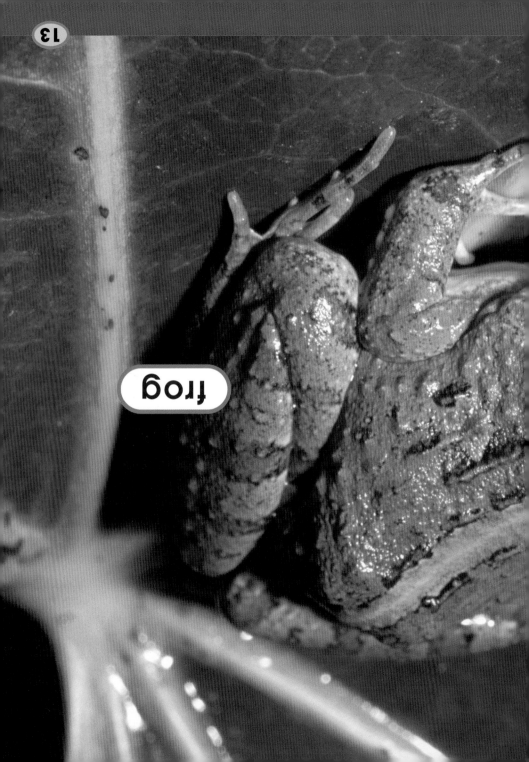

frog

Guide Notes

Title: Slimy Skin

Stage: Emergent – Magenta

Genre: Nonfiction (Expository)

Approach: Guided Reading

Processes: Thinking Critically, Exploring Language, Processing Information

Written and Visual Focus: Photographs (static images), Index, Labels

Word Count: 37

FORMING THE FOUNDATION

Tell the children that this book is about animals that have slimy skins.

Talk to them about what is on the front cover. Read the title and the author.

Focus the children's attention on the index and talk about the different animals that are in this book.

"Walk" through the book, focusing on the photographs and talk about the animals, where they are, and their slimy skins.

Read the text together.

THINKING CRITICALLY

(sample questions)

After the reading
- Why do you think these animals have slimy skins?
- Where do you think animals with slimy skins like to live?

EXPLORING LANGUAGE

(ideas for selection)

Terminology
Title, cover, author, photographs

Vocabulary
Interest words: slug, snail, worm, fish, frog
High-frequency words: this, has, a

Index